Making Way

POEMS

Making Way

Publication © Modjaji Books 2019

Text © Joan Metelerkamp 2019
First published in 2019 by Modjaji Books
modjajibooks.co.za
ISBN 978-1-928215-86-8
e-book ISBN 978-1-928215-87-5
Edited by Colleen Crawford Cousins
Cover artwork: Sonja Britz
Cover design and layout: Megan Ross

Set in Cormorant

Making Way

POEMS

Joan Metelerkamp

For my family

Metelerkamp
Maughan-Brown
McConnachie

CONTENTS

1.

Behind everything   11

This is the beginning   14

Of all the ones not yet told   17

All morning in elsewhere   20

Discernment   22

The place   23

2.

And then again	27
Emigrant	28
A wife far from home	29
Birthday	30
The stranger asks	31
This side	32
Terrace	33
Advent	34
Not every piece	36
Underside	37
Granddaughter	38
Who, where will remember us	39

3.

Ones who felt the flames	49
Don't go	50
Tree across the track	56
Wild	58
Is there anything like home now	60
Here	61
Woodhoepoes on a bookbinding course	62
Poems of the end	63
Flexi non frangi	65
Glossary	70
Acknowledgements	72
About	76

1.

Behind everything

in front of everything

now greying and softening

while at the tiny klim-op's pale florets go the white-eye's
ringed eyes the torso reaching homunculus-like

an old man in his chair dying
impossibly like his great-grand-
ambiguous amphibious now forming being

•

*o earth I am working to assemble every
day o sea turning in you to assemble*

•

all life holding in your amniotic sea
everything we are between
(little figurine)
little female phallus little figure little finger

•

crying in the shower
the sea there with the little cough of loneliness –
Lulu's first birthday! my daughter's little sea-horse's

so-far-nameless's sonar
chin mouth forehead curving in in
amniotic consciouslessness
the other side of farther   *father*
and here I am still
assembling senselessness homelessness

•

am I myself carrying
something like dying

I want to eat everything
at once want to write everything read all at once
while all I have to do is
sit still, head up, lie down, dream, cry, remember, sleep
(the dreams!)

thought I wanted to get
fit strong be
strong enough
while all I want   is

•

do I tell him
how important it is

he is dying

at home, here, even now,

I thought he was meant to show us how

thought he was suffocating me a little
heavy homunculus around my neck
now it's this grimace like a monkey baby his clinging
like a little baboon I'm seeing
I think I'm getting it at last

•

we aren't just dogs who can go off
and die quietly
in dignity under a tree
in this godforsaken February –
forget it!

forget all the injunctions, cling
as he must
to the neck of the nurse, her smile
as she slides her thick thighs
through his

all the women are needed every
day and every
son and everyman

•

"woorde van liefde, meneer"

This is the beginning

Meanwhile the seasons shift, the fish eagles call
the boubous repeat themselves

      the interruptions continue
get as far as February – give up –
March – his collapse –

"do you think I won't ever walk again"

every day like every cup of tea every spoon of sugar
you forget to stir to hold to be sipped through the straw
this is all there is, this is what there is

•

See now
with the brain at the back of the skull
the body in good use the true north just off –
little cisticola on the old sawn-off pole

longitudinal, horizontal shadows
of the other poles in this drop-dead
luminous sun

•

Now the sun won't come out again
come in, nothing left to do, wait
where the sun can't ever
come –

everything arbitrary, no authority
not that there ever really was –

his last words were and were they
his last ever

"are you still here"

•

Who will read your stuff now
if even he who never really did
if even he who never really got
what you were
doing, or thinking of not doing,
nor got what you were not –

what to do or not now he
is not, now he no longer is

•

Now you remember
this is what happens with death –

everything becomes
too much

•

The need to begin again now
 a new conception of beginning
 and end –

while he kept trying to keep you
 you to keep him   you both knew it
"what can I say"
you'd used the stock phrases
"don't go yet" "why are you in such a hurry"
and over and over, the jokes, the stories –

along the track coming back: the clear-eyed sun's
silent reminder: his long-ago counsel,
before something you had never imagined
you could do – run the cross-country –

"run! get in the front and stay there"

now, now you're learning again how to allow
glutes to release, lengthening bit by bit
latissimus dorsi into wings from the shoulder sockets,

let them!

Of all the ones not yet told

There's the one about Johanna and her grandpa –

it was a sunny day in the onderdorp
and nothing strange about my walking about
with the little box in the packet;
puddles, peels, plastic underfoot
amongst the fruit sellers and taxi stalls
loud, bright with isiXhosa and Kaaps –

he'd been with the undertaker for nearly a month
though he'd had the social dues
he'd specifically asked for
on the way back from his nephew's funeral:
the church, since the church has a roof on it,
and at the farm's celebrations, funerals and weddings,
it tended to rain and the roof to leak,
and the church is opposite the post office
and across the road
from the chemist
so easy to squeeze between
a congregation's routines –

we'd stood on the pavement and wept
after the tea, with the sisters who'd nursed him,
his grandson and I, me propped against him
as I'd leaned on his trunk in the pew;
we'd given away the rest of the scones –
but that day not to the car guard, usually there

for the wisecracks and coins
the old man liked to share –

we'd wept at the resonant
flinching-at-nothing life-telling,
one brother then the other,
 his name son's, his saw-miller son's
'n groot boom het in die bos geval –

but that was all done
and all we had to do was
take the packet I'd put in the passage,
take the symbol –
how could we know they were really his ashes,
anyone's guess, anyone's ashes –
shoe-box-size box –
bury it under the trees,
opposite the compost heap,
at the foot of the hill,
among old stones cemented back,
propped up with poles –

with him
our mother
once more
carved in stone
with us –

and why this is the one about him,
her grandpa, and Johanna:
she refused

at sixteen, at the undertakers, not to see
through the lilac grey black plastic
over-kill sentimentality –
he would burn –

untroubled by what had become
of the last neurons firing
last flare flickering
so clearly in the early-hours-depth-of-night morning
coughed up
out with all the bloody globs of the living last
of his lungs –

old log for the fire
all that was left of him, left for him to give, given,
become the fire
and the ash –

now Johanna and her cousin Heather,
pale and pink as her name-flower, in sturdy boots,
while her father in his hole-y working jersey
carried the spade, dug with it, placed the box,
under the perdepram, milkwoods,
listened to silence in silence –

Zoë, Zoë, breath of life,
in one of the old man's old button-up warmies,
and Ruth too, come back to her father's father's farm,
four of his exquisite next begotten unaware
of their hair falling like late July leaves, dun-gold,
for all of us out in the cold and open there.

All morning in elsewhere

Enough for a headache
enough for the ache in the left side, side
of the heart-cage rib-place under the left breast

where you landed when you fell
over the step as you ran for the phone
like tripped up
by history, family,
falling like in love
for what, old love,
old pulls of love?
dive into the ruck or is it the maul onto the deck –

where else, how you could live –
 how give up
 what you love

like the start of a story

    from a house on a hill by the sea

•

at the start there's nothing to be done
the foundations of this house have been built upon
Mother's suicide

just a fact of life

nothing
escapes

•

  What to do or what to not do –
  what form to turn to, to take, make
  of my life even now how to make a living –

autistic, anguished, in a hell of a mess, this is
me all over, all over again, all over the place,
come to nothing, no place

Discernment

makes its choices, reasons
through rhetoric
as well as it can;

but for Grief –
whose maiden name is written
at the turn off to the farm –
and on the covers of books – written
in the house on the hill –

and monosyllabic
first name carved
at the foot of the parents' gravestone
at the foot of the hill
among the perdepram and milkwood –

Reason, remind Grief
the one she goes with is you;
remind her, however far you take her
you can break,
like a husband's face,
into Joy.

The place

knew of you
you were loved

how could you have
not felt it,
not kept it,

you knew it,
knew its river
took the mother's

suicide like the blood of silt out to sea
washed it again
and again took it

gave back the backs of the dunes
covered with thicket
covered with bird cries

what have you left

2.

And then again

I want to hold her and kiss her and cry
as she holds her baby and kisses her and holds and holds and
I want to say! all the hurts all the smallest of hurts I have done
you! all month

all the hardest things I have said never one would I wish again
never one! too wild
and afraid too negative and abrasive

even in my throat and in my diaphragm even there I know it's
too   wild!

And outside calm and noisy and hot, noisy and busy,
and messy in this foreign street;

and the tree of the ghettos in full leaf the tree of heaven
and I know this crying is too much and that they are gone
for the morning only and her "what if anything should happen
to her"

meaning her daughter was and is as it should be and normal
and natural and this
wildness of mine as if I were immigrant, homeless, ridiculous

as the fear of dying of dying
of the too young but the old must
die
libera me!

Emigrant

In the night a Hokusai-like great wave of grief takes you
great wail pushes up through the diaphragm wakes you
to utter forgetfulness what has caused this
something absurd babble something unintelligible
cry they all hate me to your husband's wild
animal-panic-shooshing-and-soothing as if you were the horse herself dragging
your seven year old self soft side down hands along the gravel.

A wife far from home

will not tell her husband
even the names of streets
like the sewing-machine mender's street
like "Kamassie" could make her cry

trees, streets, taken for granted, given, names

like the dead and the wisdom of the dead, wasted

•

she could pray
with the bells of longing
practicing on Monday

ancient bells
ancient city once bombed to hell
every day new to her
country, walls, alleys, even trees

open me
she could pray;

across the road
walks an old woman,

holds the arm of a silent man, sings
in tune to her own discords

Birthday

Son's twenty seventh.
Wake early and sleep again wake again
make tea eat bread-and-jam for two
ibuprofen for the pain;

phone;

use the biggest truism of all
    the world
is unimaginable without you;

take your dog for a walk in the rain
come back to the house you must call home;
phone again; this time his father
in training, wherever that is;
write to two friends over there
with sons where you well know *all things fall*;

think of what's in front of you
think of how to move think
before you pick up that heavy-duty
what the movers called hoover;

look up and out of the little kitchen stable door
at the dove flying by on the ceramic tile on the brick back
                                                          wall.

The stranger asks

what you love
doing is implied,
what life does it have;

is it dead already
or has it almost died:

stuffed in its boxes
stuffed on top of the books:

Cinderellas in silks or are they so many
Bluebeard's brides –

like a daughter's old dolls waiting for a granddaughter,
porcelain legs sticking out of petticoats
coffined in their see-through boxes under the eaves –

Sleeping Beauties but somewhere over there
in the sun in the chair
the thread-bare thorn-pricked prince.

This side

You have turned around –
now you sit with your back to the sun –

not only that it blinds you
but to dry your hair –
block of sun, come back

now you confront the shelves directly:
the books cursed by the packers that side
zincwadi! zincwadi! zincwadi!
and this side the movers
fuck, no, mate, more books;

(at home, the room with the books
 opened to the river, valley, sea beyond dunes, cattle,
 boubou, chorister, brown-hooded-kingfisher,
list listed, calls listened to, into
the night the nightjar the moon
escorted out);

here, the lives are in books,
Hughes, Stevens, the reviews of your lives
read into the sleepless hours they call small –

but now! this morning –

come again sun warm with
Elizabeth Bishop's *perfectly useless concentration.*

Terrace

At last the windows above are turning
into eyes; with the dead
ivy clinging like a monobrow
down the nose of the small shed
to the rank stink of cat;

old TV aerials and ancient chimney pots
fantastical hair-dos carried straight backed and aloft;

at last a bee between the stones at the cyclamen's ears;

and the face of a clay woman
laid flat on the slabs
regards the clouds;

put a chair there and overlook
the brick yard;

at last you'll hear them:
the five incessant
syllables the calls
insistent doves call

your soul, joanie, it's
your soul's journey, it's
your turn, joanie! This

Advent

Not *that* you do but *how*
you remind yourself how not
to torment yourself with what
you are not will not ever etcetera
this is an old tune I want to say refrain
refrain
I want to say
let the reason and faith as old as *via negativa* –

let the *how* of something else
keep coming, keep it coming, capacity, *negative capability*,
a way of, of being, seeing
how – how it happens – after coming
into the kitchen, out of the cold, back to the chair,
a dog on a cushion in front of the Aga
after dreaming out of the grey though it is mid-day
and who knows how
you'll get used to it;

something bigger than will draws the curtain
back, aside, to admit
what is barely there

and it is winter! Already a long month ago
crepuscular light leapt back
into the ordinary afternoon;
no one has taught you how
to look out to the dark

whistling of crackers like bombs from another age
what are the prototypes, the archetypes, Christ!
listen to the dogs' – through the walls –
high pitched barking, ridiculously, into the cold,
listen to the kids in their coats and their heat, attentively!

Waiting, refraining, inhabiting, inhibiting panic
allow for time give time to give way give place make way.

Not every piece

                         has to be the whole story
not every day

but to keep at the odd row as if it could all grow
one day into a field full of cabbages

or more like a plain
cardigan for a granddaughter;

there's only so much looking down and sticking
to your knitting you can do;

only so much sitting in the kitchen.
But I do like the kitchen floor –

why not look at its uneven tiles
the bottom of a rock pool recalled
down at the wild side –

and the table's legs shaped
like the legs of a slender bushbuck
let them stand for a day.

Under side

Down in the kitchen – dark side
of the season closing in –

stacking the dishes tracking

the under-hum, under-thought
sound track; something close

takes traction, not tractor,
but "hanker", hankering
not just for ploughed-down ploughed-up
clods' shine,

but the length and the breadth of the whole
karoo: stones anchoring sky.

Granddaughter

As with my own children,
barely any written trace to recall
the live weight, heft
of her soft stone head
heavy on this rib-cage bed – my heart – Cora –

and all along these long months of mourning
I thought it was a place and the people
I left, who live there, who left
this imprint like the mark of sleep on a cheek –

Who, where will remember us

In front of his windows as if they belonged to him
and everything behind
the rain and the trees
as if they were there for him –
this is how my father used to sit.

Sometimes it seems I have not
come into my own yet,
then, now, to be old!
Without any ancestors here, where
shall I call home?

Did I shut him out to protect myself, how
did I shut him out?

He sat in his chair when I talked with him there, where
I talked with him almost every day,
with the celtis behind him and the fields
in front of him, the oak, and the fresh
shock of the old
stump, coral tree chopped down –

he said some things too hard for me to hear –
he said he could only get the Requiem I wrote for his wife,
                                                  the life
giver and taker,
Mother,
after the woman he loved

to flirt with wrote her article for the Times;
what was it she told him?

•

I am lying on my bed in the front room
in our little slice of row house
in this little northern city
in the South West
of this island.

I look out of this window the only window
with any aspect. Aspect.

A series of five sideways eaves and slates
of grand houses perpendicular to this street
and more than thirty five chimney pots.

In the window or out are the waving patters
of bamboo branches and leaves beyond
counting and patterning,
the window-pane running with rain streaks and beyond
the bamboo the branches
of silver birch
at the back of the big house,
across the street,
only at this angle
only the roofs and the clouds and wires
telephone or electricity
I can't tell.

On the closest eave an illegible plaque
seems to say something "Security";
letters so little and old, surely something "Society";
I can just see "Exeter."
In my mother's old binoculars the notice reads
"Venture Security".
Jesus. Is it the world, the times,
oxymorons wherever I look, not to mention morons
("considered offensive", "no longer in use";
"It is easier to become the president
of the United States than a good poet").

Leaves are gradually golding
behind the five wire lines.

•

The 11th hour of the 11th month –
everywhere, for a minute, silenced –

led from their lives lined up
against the wall of the war –

from everywhere you walk here,
everywhere we walk
each village we come across –
many rivers and many voices,
hills crossed with many hedges of many species –
names, crosses;
under the ashes at Upton Pyne,
at least four Elises –

remember, remember the calls of children's voices!
Look into prams' and pushcarts'
fat little sleeping faces;
other crosses, other village places,
like right in this city, this Heavitree,
hanging, burning of witches –

not to forget .

I went with my father after my mother
laid down her life
up against her bedroom wall,
let the scarlet thread unravel
into morning's black rivulet
away from us all –
I went in her place, to what we called Santie's funeral,
where fifty five years before
into the obdurate face of the fog-veiled mountains
he flew his crew.
Santie, Alexander, one of the names of the brothers,
my father's cousins, at home,
in the little church,
under the milkwoods and cape ash,
on the brass plaque,
the cool stone wall.

We stood, my father and I, in the midst
of that small gathering in the mist
 among stones, rocks and old bits of plane
with the old fighters he'd died flying to feed –
in their alpine hats, their alpine soft cragged faces,

the old resistance fighters and my father
in his red maroon rain coat and his own stooping hat,
made our commemoration procession
down the flanks of the Alps with flags
for a service of thanks for his spirit.
Behind the South African ambassador
the list as long as the building's façade –
all the boys of this little Italian village
lost in Russia, lost in Russia, lost in Russia
(and Kosovo then close across the border);
and the son of the other brother, plane shot down
somewhere over the desert, who didn't ever know his father,
came many years later for my father's funeral
 so after the church we had to go back to the groot huis
 to open the wine;
(which my father – having drunk so much he fell asleep
with the farming music, the pastoral, the slow movement,
the bath running over, while he kept an eye
on the apple of that eye, his name-son –
would have approved;
he swam through to the other side
of his own deep
drinking
like when the river came up
his second son swam
over the fields to fetch his cows)

•

In our house on the hill on that farm
there lives a strange man

I'm afraid I don't know
if I dare write, if I can really tell
why I'm afraid –
in our house, on a hill, by the sea,
the part of the farm my father left us,
there is a locked door.

On the part of the farm my father left my brother
this brother milks his cows. He bends over his vats
and stirs his cheese. He tends his fields.
He looks after everyone and his dogs,
employs two men and perhaps three part-time women,
he's fluent in four African languages
one of which is English.
Sooner or later no-one will care.

•

If I think wishfully
           although I'm almost 60
 I want, I also want, to live until I'm 90.

I want to sit in a window of light
             and write. To be able to draw
I would love

but you don't need to tell me
             how much work
so I'll just turn to lines

 late-gold
    and various shades of greeny-
pinky-pale

I come my love
    to make tender
arms of birches

gentle as the people's voices
    and skin
soft as babies' faces.

3.

Ones who felt the flames

whether you were
      or were not
        there –

brothers who felt the flames
in the early hours far gone

who woke to flames and fought them
and moved the cattle first, first milked them –

your father's house, your sister's house, your own tall trees –

the tarconanthus fragrance
the sea beyond
everything you have held close inside
the river the valley
the fish eagles' arms of wide blessing and cry

place on earth   you knew,
               cousin, children, friends
    you had no
hold on earth –

Don't go

no, no, *not to Lethe*

remember

go down to the streams of panic
since you must but remember

something called
soul is waiting for you

you risk failure you fail you fail
to bring it back

to consciousness

you know you need to
look up look out forward
remember walking by yourself

before you were lost in the crowds going down underground

when they say you failed and you believed them you failed
you looked back you used their words ones you heard
like "the book is a dud" you couldn't trust
you were bringing it up to consciousness

you couldn't remember

soul couldn't look up look out through his eyes look at the length

of his back
at the back of his legs as he walks forward keep walking forward

call   tell him you are still here
he may not see
you may actually have to work
 move
don't just stand there like a forsaken fucking shadow

 like you don't don't you
        believe me

•

The house, the road, the dunes, trees, fynbos
from Groenvlei to the mouth of the Goukamma

but the dread long before
since it was
unimaginable

you hadn't imagined every path all paths engulfed you'd imagined
exile and cunning
along tracks

mongoose porcupines shrews rats
lizards dungbeetles cobra duiker bush-buck bushpig rooikat
boomslang   dune mole-rats

spiders spiders   butterflies

moths

moths

stick-

insects

worms

myriad birds you no longer hear nor incessant syllables of frogs

•

smoke screen or merciful mist off the sea
(like the poet wrote in his book for me
somewhere in there the god is hiding)

•

and the fire came

I mean the message came

we weren't asleep we were rustling, whispering

the berg wind again and we hadn't even heard

(how many nights we'd stood on the stoep
or just in the passage, imagining,
sniffing)

but now it was light
like the morning after the night
mother shot herself –
I mean heard on the phone –

could not save

flames leapt the road

        your house gone

resources pulled out from under me –

tried to close the south-western flank

trying to save Ganzvlei

N2 closed –

by the time he phoned, fire at the gate –

milked the cows first can you believe –

klapped an inyoni behind the shed –

huh?

burning bit of debris   incendiary –

sorry sorry –

so sorry   totally –

is it still burning –

totally   to the sea –

present continuous and everything you aren't holding
in
this
minute
you are getting the message
                         sinking it in
for how many nights you are waking sweating lurching as if you
stopped breathing

imagine
flinging your body   across the hill
as if   as if
you could hold it back bring it back through its burnt through skin
sticks and sand like a mother's dead body and

a father's little O of a mouth
you stood stiff and still beside

(and how it is in the graveyard amongst the milkwoods
 at the foot of the hill
cover your waxed-in ears and your cataract-eyes
nothing can tell)

•

weeks of weakness, weeks of sleeplessness,
weeks of swollen feet,
unbending back, don't look back, *she don't look back*,
back to this back to back whisper
with first dove call, pre-dawn call,
through the blinds with the wind
are you asleep
come back to consciousness
I wish   no   are you   should I go back   should you –

•

look up   see the faces over the water

in their still moving photos in their funerary canoes
children suspend their disbelief
like paddles over the black
water *the stubborn river of woe*
old-man's-beard dripping from milkwoods
shadows of ripples of
long ago afternoon shade after
mother's memorial tea

look up   this is what I see

Tree across the track

They forget I knew it long before

well before each hoisted beam and truss
purlin   joists for floorboards   to be laid across

              fynbos   thicket   sky and sea
through wall-less frames   open window spaces

to the river doubled-back and beyond

to the mouth   to the sea

psorolea   freesia   wild camphor
in the wind   fragrances
dusty dry   kooigoed   helichrysum

the other side of the seasons   spring
cuckoos at it piet-my-vrou now starting
like Klaas's "meitjie" or "I'm- so-siiiick"

at the foot of the hill   start at the graveyard
opposite the compost heap
just behind that little house

whitewashed
house in the valley where the faithful still live
orange trees   blossom   beginning   monkeys leaping
back into milkwood and perdepram

follow the brown-hooded kingfisher
guide to how to catch what's right in front of you
or the free whistle of the sombre bulbul
or at last the little goshawk threading through
stumps of thicket in the flank of this track

where the electricity cable is coming out of its casing
if it survived at all like the puffadder
who slithers its spring obesity   stand still   take time

listen   you think you can hear the sea   you can
fish eagle   yes

go on   beyond this turn on the hill
where there's a rooikrans that somehow avoided the flames
blown across the track   on   further

follow the little bushbuck doe
or maybe if you're lucky the rooikat

maybe they'll be coming back
to the top
where you can see forever

the fire

    the end of the world

Wild

Not just the house with its winter hearth,
but my wild side too –

like the beach at the mouth of the river
(ox-bow through the valley below us,
the gold-brown sluggish, brackish
snake of the river, Goukamma)
on the wild side, the rocks and cross currents
 (wrecked the carrier-ship, spilt the panic);
but on the other, littoral miles of sand and
pungence of dune-bush, surf-spray
drifting to nothing –

over the threshold, as I opened the door,
in the house on the hill, I stepped over
the boomslang, making me re-think God again –

often in the dusk smudge of thicket
or in morning's absolute clear:
traces – spine of porcupine, stink of skunk,
shy shadow of darling my mongoose, pitched ear of lynx –

the gift of earth and heaven-sent
place that place gives –

how can I not look back like the one who looked back
in wild forgetfulnes and forever lost it –

•

all authenticity, authority,
the voices of the forefathers,
the old man in the valley
with not enough oxygen to the brain;
his sons, his name-son,
without
everything
recalling family
history, books, photos, letters, paintings, forefathers'
stinkwood chairs, mother's embroidered seats,
all, all the ancestors called
"wêreld se goed"–

his house, home, his life-work, the work of his forebears,
creation and recreation,
farm fields sheds, wood-working tools, machines, vehicles –
entire saw-mill razed

300 people without employment
30 years planning, building, meticulous counting, raising
hell   raging
fire   fighting
across the mountain
forest   river gorge

still he is
the ones he saved   are
we all dispersed   are
blessed with the mother of all after-death aftermath

Is there anything like home now

said the swallow, packing mud at the eaves,
where on earth should I be

here, in the middle of sat-nav's confusion,
hedges, single-lane lanes leading the wrong way
on hard surfaced tracks, diffusion

like sun into cataract eyes, field
after lit field, Bright Field
of England, ancient Pearl and Piers Plowman,
did you bring me here?

•

When, wept the owl, will I
know something,
be somewhere, where
they know who I am at least,
names, words, where, when, make sense,
like a mouse in the smeuse;

from this ancient bearu,
across the leigh
I'll look out and I'll think
ash, ash, beech, birch,
in your shade, in your limbs, yes
trees are getting to know me.

Here

Examining the excel spread sheets
through the supermarket specs
now that the cataract is out

the right eye keeps weeping
the figures keep dancing –
red shoes they can't take off –

nothing in place, nothing at home, given
the scorched earth gift
of manic destruction;

but here, when it's not all only costs,
returns that won't tally,
hear the cold note of the owl in the ash

like the low call of the far off fluff-tail
in the long-gone so-called
nights of the soul

Woodhoepoes on a bookbinding course

Here is a tree –
red berries, compound leaves, not tall –

from its branches poems
spin in cardboard strips,
dream catchers, wind catchers,
little propellors, paper planes
with the wings of words –

little rowan tree, with your flock of poems,
long tails dangling loose
like bushveld hlekabafasi in the sun –

women are laughing in the sun –

when we are gone, always
you will have let
light words alight
amongst the well worn ones of Devon
sounding their zwer
"like a covey of partridges taking off"

Poems of the end

I am this side, outside
under the stricken ash
allowing its leaves, easily, naturally –

poems come, rise all day, shaking free
as a cat from the grass or the smell of grass itself
freedom itself –

somewhere Tsvetaeva seeds "I didn't want this"
coming like weeds, intersticially,
between the lines like Akhmatova's long line of mothers
in the snow outside the prison "can you describe this" –
yes. Yes. Her assurance, her will,
she didn't wait for words to come to her
as "woman much missed how you call to me"
called to me, under the celtis –

cut kikuyu, clatter of sink-plaat,
hot roof expanding like patter of early rain
your side, hemisphere, your farm,
free writing coming clear as the presence
of a suicide grandmother I had never known
 – after the end of all that – as if it ever comes to an end –
and often with these poets, although I didn't know it,
more than comrades, more like figures of psyche,
animus soul figures, as if something could endure,

as if all weren't only moment
by moment and sometimes, suddenly, epiphany –

Mxolisi, Vonani, Lesego, and deeply, utterly Angifi,
though we were only once or twice all together with you there
Seitlhamo's "River Robert" *we are at peace here*
we bless the mysteries and the silence

as here, under this English ash,
the scratch of the nib and sleeve
in little increments across the page
as the scratch, scratch of your karree,
growing too close, against the pane.

"Flexi non frangi"

> *for us, like any other fugitive*
> *it is today in which we live*

Even then, even in the end

you'll never know
you've got to   the end

disappearing like an old man looking up
from the bloody offal of his coughed up lungs:
"are you still here?"

Once
there was
the long time of now
                and then

it comes to you as sudden as the swarm itself
sudden swarm through every crevice into the house with
the berg wind
hot in the middle of winter or just-spring
the cloud of bees detonating
against the panes

season of boomslangs and puffadders –

don't ask why
this should come to you –

in *perfectly useless concentration* widening
the vision of happiness, freedom, freeing
as the purpose and end – telos –
come like the advent of a child longed for
to pour all your love for

bees   breaking   free –
with the scent of tarconanthus'
camphor,
bitter buchu, sweet of psorolea,
trace of salt wind dropped to breeze off the sea –

free from –
but what to –

not the old freedom of the comrades, comrade,
not any freedom to fight for
no more
"if you're not for us you're against us!"

arising like the sound of bees
like the coming of a poem
the smell of bees
like sweaty socks,
under the floorboards honey, honey,
wax sweating in the planks in the walls, in the walls

the queen
at her regeneration
workers searching
to keep her

making their way
in through the cracks –

Rasta boy-man on the apex of the roof
like an Indian god, his straight back strong,
limbs wheeling free,
stings, thick smoke, smoking out, tar
messy down the roof sheets where internal walls are –

where did the swarm swarm
to become itself
a vast nest, shelter, sheltering
in the wild pear (dombeya) – *honey bees, come build*

where no one believed
freedom, spirit, scraped out
like so much blighted ovum, old moulded beeswax .

The house burnt now like the ground
to the ground and now
only the chimney like in the plantation, the forest, there
chimneys, foundations, sometimes, still, concrete floors,

(old ones
gone to the city,
trekked to another country)

the place, the whole
hill abandoned.

End: as in purpose: beginning

to see again
don't throw the tender inception out
with the waters of doubt –

end as in always
beginning, learning again to free
not into Freedom but freer than before
not every day but every day
learning to not restrict

"one muscle one body"

bending not breaking bending
from the top of the femur allowing
the spine its length, strength –

remember the old man, at home,
before his last fall his last
"do you think I'll never walk again",
down in the valley, as if it were a decree,
"you are free my daughter", and again,
as if in benign benison, "free" –
 and carved in plain wood on the stoep,
plain for all to see, crest of the family
"flexi non frangi" –

all burnt, all gone, all up in flames –

immigrant,
fugitive, refugee

old, old story
old as the words

you have come to
old as silence you can't hear yourself think through –

amongst these ashes, now, this foreign
birdsong, these gentle strangers,
this old stone .

GLOSSARY

klim-op – a creeper poisonous to cattle

woorde van liefde meneer – love-words, sir

boubous – shrikes who sing "synchronised duets" in pairs

onderdorp – the poorer area of the town's business district

'n groot boom het in die bos geval – literally: a huge tree has fallen in the forest

perdepram – a "knobwood" tree (literal translation – horse's teats)

kamassie – a small evergreen in the understory of afromontane forest, particularly the Tsitsikamma

izincwadi – books

groot huis – the main house on a farm (literally a "big house")

boomslang – a deadly poisonous snake; "tree snake"

rooikat – lynx

klap – hit

inyoni – bird

kooigoed – literally "bedding stuff" as this species of helichrysum was used for bedding in the past

wêreld se goed – worldly goods

piet-my-vrou – red-chested cuckoo, named after its call

Klass's meitjie – the call of Klaas's cuckoo is on 2 notes sounding like "meitjie" meaning maid

"I'm so si-iick" – the call of the black cuckoo

inhlekabafazi – green wood-hoopoe (literally: "the laughter of women" from the cackling sound the birds make; they are usually found in groups; breeding birds are helped by the group, chicks being fed by all group members)

kikuyu – a grass particulalry good for grazing, hay or silage.

sinkplaat – corrugated iron

rooikrans – an invasive acacia, from Australia, cultivated originally for dune stabilisation in South Africa

smeuse – a little gap in the hedge

bearu – forest

leigh – field

zwer – sound made by partridges taking off

flexi non frangi – bend don't break

§

Mxolisi Nyezwa, Vonani Bila, Lesego Rampholokeng, Angifi Dladla are four well known South African contemporary poets who have taken part in readings and workshops organised by the poet Robert Berold in the small city formerly known as Grahamstown (now Makhanda). Robert Berold has also, over the years, organised many gatherings of poets and writing students on his farm outside Makhanda; he is the publisher of Deep South books.

ACKNOWLEDGEMENTS

"A new conception if beginning and end"
– D.H.Lawrence

"all things fall"
– W.B.Yeats

"perfectly useless concentration"
– Elizabeth Bishop

"I come my love"
– William Carlos Williams

"No no go not to Lethe"
– John Keats

"the stubborn river of woe"
– Galway Kinnell

"somewhere in there the god is hiding"
– Alasdair Patterson

"exile and cunning"
– James Joyce

"she don't look back"
– Bob Dylan

> *"woman much missed, how you call to me, call to me"*
> – Thomas Hardy

> *"we are at peace here/we bless the mysteries and the silence"*
> – Seitlhamo Motsapi

> *"for us like any other fugitive/ it is today in which we live"*
> – W.H. Auden

> *"honey bees, come build"*
> – W.B. Yeats

§

Most of the poets quoted or referred to in this book are men (and I thank Robert Berold for his reading of this book as manuscript). The women poets and readers whose presence is less overt in the text are for the most part contemporaries and ones whose influence has been more direct, personal and immediate. So, though the poems do not overtly acknowledge them I thank: Colleen Crawford Cousins for her detailed editorial reading; Colleen Higgs as ever for everything (including also editorial input) that goes into the publishing of a Modjaji book; Marike Beyers and Jo-Ann Bekker for reading the manuscript at various stages; and Nancy Campbell, Sue Boyle and Fiona Benson for comments on single poems.

I also particularly thank my daughter Frances for keeping on believing in, and reminding me of, the place of pattern in our lives; and Sonja Britz for the use of her rich and suggestive painting 'Automne' on the cover of this book

"Behind Everything", appeared in *Stanzas*, "And then again" and a version of "Terrace" in a selection of South African poems for the US based *Illuminations*; versions of "Who will remember", "Underside" and "Ones who felt the flames" in *New Coin*.

ABOUT JOAN METELERKAMP

This is Joan Metelerkamp's ninth book of poems. Her previous book, also published by Modjaji, *Now the World Takes these Breaths* (2014) was one of three on the short list for the Glenna Luschei Prize for African Poetry. Her poems have appeared in many South African anthologies. As well as poems she has written reviews and essays about South African poetry, and read in most festivals in South Africa as well as in Lisbon, Rio de Janeiro and Paris. She has been an associate of the Institute for the Study of English in Africa, as a part-time teacher on the MA in creative writing at Rhodes University; before that, for five years, she edited *New Coin* poetry journal.

Having left Knysna where she lived on a family farm for twenty years she is currently living with her husband in Devon UK training to be a teacher of the Alexander Technique.

www.ingramcontent.com/pod-product-compliance
Lightning Source LLC
Chambersburg PA
CBHW011952150426
43196CB00019B/2921